Resume Writing 2016: Get the Job You Actually Want

An Ultimate Guide on Resume Writing and Tips to Win You Your Dream Job

Table of Contents

Introduction

Chapter 1- Essentials to Successfully Land a New Job

Chapter 2- Surefire Qualities of a Job Winning Resume

Chapter 3- How to Write a "Selling" Cover Letter

Chapter 4- Why you Should Have a LinkedIn Profile

Chapter 5- Why a Personal Website Distinguishes You from the "Crowd"

Chapter 6- The Social Media: What Should You Know?

Chapter 7- Does Volunteering for Vocational Services Help?

Chapter 8- Preparing for your First Interview

Conclusion

Thanks again for downloading this book, I hope you enjoy it!

© Copyright 2016 by Alpha Lifestyle Productions - All rights reserved.

This document is geared towards providing exact and reliable information in regards to the topic and issue covered. The publication is sold with the idea that the publisher is not required to render accounting, officially permitted, or otherwise, qualified services. If advice is necessary, legal or professional, a practiced individual in the profession should be ordered.

- From a Declaration of Principles which was accepted and approved equally by a Committee of the American Bar Association and a Committee of Publishers and Associations.

In no way is it legal to reproduce, duplicate, or transmit any part of this document in either electronic means or in printed format. Recording of this publication is strictly prohibited and any storage of this document is not allowed unless with written permission from the publisher. All rights reserved.

The information provided herein is stated to be truthful and consistent, in that any liability, in terms of inattention or otherwise, by any usage or abuse of any policies, processes, or directions contained within is the solitary and utter responsibility of the recipient reader. Under no circumstances will any legal responsibility or blame be held against the publisher for any reparation, damages, or monetary loss due to the information herein, either directly or indirectly.

Respective authors own all copyrights not held by the publisher.

The information herein is offered for informational purposes solely and is universal as so. The presentation of the information is without a contract or any type of guarantee assurance.

The trademarks that are used are without any consent, and the publication of the trademark is without permission or backing by the trademark owner. All trademarks and brands within this book are for clarifying purposes only and are the owned by the owners themselves, not affiliated with this document.

Introduction

I want to thank you and congratulate you for downloading the book, "Resume Writing: Get the Job you Actually Want."

This book contains proven steps and strategies on how to write a selling resume and cover letter that will win you your dream job.

Equipped with strategies on how to sell your accomplishments and success both online and in hard copy documents, this book will offer you with top notch information on how to give the first impression to your employer that will create a long lasting impression. **Highlighted here are the topics to expect:**

- Resume tips and tricks;

- Creating a professional LinkedIn account;

- Social media hacks that will sell your success and accomplishments;

- What you have been doing in the wrong way that halts you from getting a job;

- Personal website and job search;

- Interview tips and tricks. And much more!

Each and every step in this guide has been backed with real like examples from people who applied them and landed on their dream jobs. As you use this guide, make an effort to iteratively improve the required areas, whether it is your accomplishments or credentials.

Thanks again for downloading this book, I hope you enjoy it!

Chapter 1: Essentials to Successfully Land a New Job

To get anywhere with your employment search, you will be required to put in a lot of time and effort. Some decades ago with just a college education and some skills, you could land a very paying job with an ultimate financial security. This trend is no more, many people are getting educated. We now have millions of college degrees, thousands of Philosophy Doctorates, and hundreds of well-educated and skills people who eye the same job that you want to apply.

Across the globe, the rate of unemployment is very high. Year around more and more people get into the job market. Such trend can easily make a potential job applicant too lazy around and lose hope due to unending disappointments from the previous job applications. We have moved to an era where knowledge isn't the only tool to land on your dream job. You got to be wise and wiser. If you are looking get anywhere in life, you will need to put maximum efforts day in day out. It also applies with job search. The following are top notch essentials to landing a great job as per experts:

1. **A Short and Succinct Resume:**

Many reports have recently claimed that employers are ruling out resumes as part of a successful job application. According to experts, resumes are part and parcel of successful job application. They form a very essential tool in the search of employment. The career experts, however, say that hiring managers are always in a rush when scrutinizing and going through job applications. Hence, there is need to format your resume in such a way that it can be read very quickly and also in small chunks.

In the current world, hiring managers scan through resumes within ten seconds. Focus in eliminating filler words. In case you want to quantify your impressive results, consider using numbers. Also, add some relevant keywords that had appeared in the job posting. You should also limit your contact information to one phone number, LinkedIn profile URL, and one email address. Use the contemporary Gmail rather than the old-fashioned AOL. There is no need of adding a residential address but it is wise to include your region like New York Tri-State. This way, the employer will be aware that you are near the location of the open position.

2. **A Profile of Job-Search Documents:**

Best job search tricks entails the art of finding ways through which you can distinguish yourself from the crowd. You should consider supplementing your resume with something that will serve as a very great advantage on the job that you are applying. Something that will make the hiring manager go for you and not the other hundreds of applications. As per Career Brainstorming Day pros, you can add collateral leadership briefs, one-page executive summaries, or blogs that establish your robust professional identity, on your resume.

3. **Perfecting Your Video Interview Skills:**

Due to the robust job applications that hiring managers receive, they opt for Skype video for initial screening. The move both serves for the initial screening and long-distance interview. To excel in video presentation, there will be a need for getting a coach. Coaches assist in perfect you in the area and thus you will handle the video interview with confidence.

4. **An Excellent LinkedIn Profile:**

The use of a LinkedIn profile in seeking employment has moved from being an added advantage to something essential. A career expert, Kursmark, says that having an excellent LinkedIn profile might be more significant than having a great resume. However, research reveals that most of the job candidates have failed to embrace this critical tool.

Furthermore, you shouldn't just curate your LinkedIn profile and sit down and wait till you apply for your next job. Always consider engaging with your networks. Make it active. Focus on your career field while using it. You can participate in interest groups and the LinkedIn industry. On your LinkedIn homepage, you can click on the "groups directory" or "groups you may like" tabs, to get relevant groups. Share information that maybe helpful and participate in discussions. Through this, you will improve the likelihood of getting noticed by hiring managers, referral sources, and recruiters.

5. **The Twitter and Other Social Media Sites:**

The social media has been reduced to a place where teenagers and youths post selfies, their daily escapades, and gossips among other memes. Although, such potential job candidates fail to understand that recruiters can use such sites as a potential job screening avenue. Actually, some employers have moved to an internal hiring process, which depends heavily on the identification of prospective employees through their online presence and referral links of the past employers. As such, you should focus more on using your social media site to improve your area of expertise and less to share your daily life escapades.

These are just but the most important essentials that will help you to land a new job. The subsequent chapters will expound on them. You will learn how to improve your Twitter presence, how to make a personal website, curating your LinkedIn profile, and making a great resume among others. Also focus on limiting the amount of time that you spend on the job boards.

It is wise to focus on your career path entirely. Put effort on what you want to do or be in life. Ask yourself what you are good at or what you want to do. In case you are good in design, focus on career and job opportunities in the design field. You should avoid 'jumping' from one field to the other. Improve yourself by reading more on your area of specialization and write to improve your presence in the job market.

Chapter 2: Surefire Qualities of a Job Winning Resume

A great resume sets you among the top candidates during the recruitment process. Many first time job applicants rough-up their resumes in an hour and proceed to apply for jobs. But, such applicants end up with disappointments as their resumes show lack of expertise both in content and skills. In any case, those who sort for expert advice and professional assistance when writing their resumes end up landing on their dream jobs within the first application.

A job winning resume has got some unique features. Most of such characteristics have been mentioned before and you can get them by simply Google Searching. You will find the regular information about reading through the resume to identify typos and grammar errors. You will also get advice like how to best format your resume depending with your career field.

Many potential job applicants end up in dilemmas on whose advice they should go with. They wonder whether they should go by their hiring managers' advice, HR's, recruiters', or professional resume writers' advice. All offer good advice but their views differ in one way or another. Although, I will go by the advice of the person who will invite you in the interview. He/she is the person who knows. These are in most cases the resume reviews in the HR department.

There are specific rules on writing very effective resumes. You should pay attention on such rules when writing your resume. **To offer you with the best chance of success in your future job** application, consider paying attention to the following ten things:

1. **Quantifiable Results**

In most cases, employers never pat attention to grocery list of roles. Rather, such employers are drawn to specific accomplishment that can be quantified with percentages, dollars, and numbers.

2. **Avoid Unsubstantiated Adaptive Skills**

In the current era, you should focus much on showing and less on telling when crafting your resume. Avoid clichés and unsubstantiated adaptive skills. Be very innovative. Find out what makes you more innovative and include them in your resume. Have you ever developed a program for your township that reduced violence by a percentage? Great, put it in your resume.

3. **Tailor Your Resume to Match That Job**

Employers get annoyed with the "copy-and-paste" type resume. It is a type of resume that can be termed as 'one-size-fits-all' resume. Such resume doesn't follow the job description or address the employer's needs. It is kind of insulting. You should always start your resume a fresh when applying for new jobs. Ensure that the resume has been tailored to match the job description and what the employer is looking for.

4. Show Relevance in Your Resume

In most cases, employers will be interested with the past ten years of your work life. Whether you have been in work for 20 or 30 years, always make sure that you have put much focus on the last 10 to 15 years. Sometimes, age discrimination can come out as a concern.

5. Include Relevant Keywords

For the occupations which are technical in nature, keywords are very essential. Ensure that you have included keywords as much as possible throughout your resume. This also applies to the job board faithful's. They should have keywords peppered in their resumes. They differentiate between being found at the top of the favorite candidates or at the bottom.

6. **Size Matters**

Employers get hundreds of resumes in a single job application. So, you should do them a favor and submit a short and thoroughly written resume. Generally, a resume should be about two pages. This is provided that you have the accomplishments and experience to back up the resume. You will need extensive experience to write a longer resume. Actually, in some cases of fresh graduates' job applicants, a single page resume will work.

7. **Understand That the Employers Never Cares of Your Needs**

Yes, employers mostly care about what they need and want. You can solve their problems by showing that you care about their needs in the resume. Make them look great and they will love you to be part of their team. As such, consider dropping the meaningless objective statements that normally reads, "I am looking for a position in a progressive firm where I can apply my journalism skills." You can substitute this with statements like, 'With my skills in journalism, I am ascertained that I will help your firm achieve its mission of being the best ranked news firm nationally."

8. **You Should Begin Your Resume with a Punch**

Below your contact information and name lies your title that serves as your brand. With about 130 characters, you can easily capture the employer's attention by starting with what you do and in which capacity. Rather than writing 'lazy' titles like "General Manager," you can come up with a branding title like "General Store Manager committed to maximizing profitability and enhancing customer service."

9. **Make it Easy to Read**

Your resume should be both visually readable and visually appealing. In most cases, employers who get hundreds of resumes, will skim/glance at them for about 6 to 10 seconds before making a decision on whether to read or not to read them at length. Your resume should be easily scannable. You should write shorter word blocks and use bullets.

10. **Wow Your Employer**

In your professional profile section, consider using WOW statements in the form of your accomplishments. Grab your employer's attention with quantifiable accomplishments. For instance, you can say, "I volunteered to assume the roles of website design and development, while still excelling at Public Relations, which resulted in $30,000 savings for the firm. Such WOW statements will motivate the resume reviewer to read on.

These tips will raise your chances of being selected as the favorite candidate for the job. Always remember that while you are seeking this kind of advice, other potential job applicants are also seeking the same advices. Therefore, there is need to focus on how you can have as many accomplishments as possible, even if it means volunteering. Also, you can include links that will direct your potential employer to your accomplishments that relate to their job position.

Chapter 3: How to Write a "Selling" Cover Letter

The most important task of a cover letter is securing you with a job interview. You will get noticed by using specific tools when crafting your CV cover letter. You should consider your cover letter as the most vital marketing tool for your CV/resume. On average, a recruitment agent will spend about 25 seconds while scanning over your cover letter for keywords that are relevant to the job post.

Your main objective will be met, provided the keywords that have been identified in your cover letter are relevant to the advertised job. Take notice of the tips and tricks below to ensure that you cover letter and CV get noticed by even the busiest recruitment agent. When writing the cover letter, there is a need of concentrating on both the personal and functional message that you will communicate. The functional message should be made of accurate information and delivered in an impactful and engaging approach.

On the other hand, the personal message should be descriptive but yet compressed. You should use the personal message to express your proficiency and professionalism. Ensure that the message exhibits a positive approach and a confidence character. Consider finding clues that might be hidden in the job advert and proceed by relating these values in your job application – specifically the cover letter. The following rules will help you when writing a CV cover letter. With them, you will notice the difference in the call backs you receive for interviews.

1. **The CV Cover Letter Title.**

The title of your job application cover letter should start with an action verb. They are also referred to as power words. Action verbs effectively illustrate your perceptions in the statements that you make. Usage of such words in titling your cover letter for job applications help in delivering a more impactful message. For instance, such a title can be: A Custom Prepared CV Cover Letter, or Professionally Written Cover Letter, or Proficiently Prepared Cover Letter.

2. **Cover Note Presentation and Layout.**

Foremost, in case you are planning to submit a hand delivered job application, use a standard A$ white paper for the cover letter. Never try to stand out of the crowd by using wild fonts and multi-colored papers. The presentation of your cover letter should be kept neutral and tidy. Always follow a professional letter layout: Begin by left aligning your contact information, address, your name, and the date (which should be on its own line). You should proceed by skipping a line and start by addressing the recipient – the content should be aligned to the right. It should encompass, the recipient's name, their designation, and the company. Finally, consider skipping one line and personally address the letter to the required recipient, E.g Dear Miss/Mrs/Mr, Dear Sir/Ma'am.

3. **Format of the Cover Letter.**

You should always keep back in your mind that when writing your cover letter, you are addressing yourself to a real person. Find out the "target audience" by paying attention to the hints that are found in the job advert. You should proceed by making attempts to talk to that person. Proceed by formatting the cover letter after preparing the basic layout.

The first paragraph should detail the position that you are applying to and the location where you found the job advert. It should be done clearly and concisely. This should be followed by an 'elevation sentence' that comprises of an impactful statement that details why your application is relevant – it shouldn't be more than a sentence. The body of your cover letter should follow in anew paragraph or two – the rules have been detailed in the 'fourth rule' below. You should finally close your cover letter with a summarized content (just one short but detailed paragraph) which details succinctly what sets you apart from all the other applicants. You should thank the recipient for their time and then close the letter respectfully with your regards, name, and contact details.

4. **Content of the Cover Letter**

The content of your cover letter is mainly the body. It is what will directly sell your CV and job application. It is always wise to ensure that the information that you provide in this section directly expresses both your transferable skills and your relevant accomplishments. The use of power words (action verbs) will clearly describe your experience and understanding of specific fields, depending on the job position.

To unmistakably illustrate your achievements, you should consider the use of quantifiable examples. You will have unambiguously communicated your success with the measurable results. The above information should be accompanied with a summary of your understanding about the company. You should also show your interest of joining the firm. Showing your understanding and knowledge about the firm reveals to the reader (resume review) that your skills compliment the culture of the organization.

5. **You Should Be Proactive in Your Cover Letter**

Before closing your cover letter, consider suggesting a possible date that you could meet with the HR agent (or recruitment agent) for an interview. Unless provided in the job post, I suggest that you count ten days from the application date. You should use that date as your prosed interview date. You should use your cover letter as a perfect opportunity to showcase your efficiency and passion. Edit and proofread your cover letter for grammatical errors and spelling mistakes.

Be sure to regularly check the contact information that you have provided. The phone should always be switched on, while you should check the email three times a day. In case you are required to respond by email or phone, be polite and professional. Do it within an hour of receiving the email. You should smile while you speak on the phone.

Sticking with above rules is an assurance that you will have grabbed the recruitment consultant's attention. It is always vital to sell your accomplishments and skills in a succinct yet persuasive way. Remember, you have got only 15 to 20 seconds to display a sticky impression. This is why you have to make use of each and every asset that you have functioning in your favor.

Chapter 4: Why You Should Have a LinkedIn Profile

A great resume and cover letter will not guarantee you that job if you are not active in LinkedIn and other social networks. During the first year when LinkedIn was unveiled, it was much optional to have a profile with them that could act as a way of displaying your resume and engaging in different groups. Today, most employers will ask you for a LinkedIn profile ULR during the job interview. Actually, some expect you to include the same in your resume.

Having an active LinkedIn profile, where you are engaging with other people in your career field, reveals a lot to the employer. The power of LinkedIn is networking. It differs with other social networks like Facebook from the fact that LinkedIn concentrates much about jobs. At present, LinkedIn has over 180 million users globally. Over half of them are happily employed. Some are unemployed while others are seeking 'greener pastures'.

An active profile with LinkedIn tells your employer that you like your career field. It also tells that you like expounding more about your career apart from being great in social networking on matters relating to your jobs. Furthermore, you will meet potential employers or people who can redirect you to potential employers. It is much like a job board, where our profile acts like a resume. Being active on LinkedIn is a great impression when searching for job. Even before applying for your next job, it is ideal to frequent on LinkedIn regularly. Here are five reasons on why you should take LinkedIn with much seriousness:

1. **A Large Network.**

Imagine you was employed and then get retrenched indefinitely with 7 people in your LinkedIn link. You will suddenly realize that you would have better capitalized a lot in getting to meet people on your network. This means that you will begin to add new members senselessly. In turn, LinkedIn will either blacklist you for this suspicious behavior or the new members whom you have invited to your network will remain with lots of questions about your intentions.

Some might think. "Have not heard from him for since college, now that he has no job and want us to connect. What might he be wanting from me? This also applies to those who are looking for jobs, it is ideal to start interacting with your LinkedIn network while still in college. It is like digging your well long before you start drinking from it. You will get to enjoy a large network that can be helpful when looking for that job. Provide value. Stay in touch. Be active.

2. **Opportunities (Maybe Passive Candidates from Recruiters).**

Some companies hire recruiters when they looking for "passive candidates." These are people who are not actively looking for a job. They are not unemployed people – although, you might be lucky and get the job despite being unemployed. Remember, they wouldn't have needed to hire a recruiter if they were looking for candidates who are unemployed. Mainly because they are plenty of such people in the job market.

Actually, such a recruiter is being paid to plunder and steal from another competitive company. They are paid to convince other happily employed people that the "grass is greener" on the other side. As a result they end up getting huge commissions from the hire. Such companies will pay you much and offer you with best services that what you are being offered with where you are presently working. In case you aren't on

LinkedIn, you will be reducing the chances of being recognized by such recruiters. This also applies to those people who are newly looking for a job.

3. **Connection and Value.**

LinkedIn has got industry groups that have really matured over time. The content shared by members is improving in quality, where members aren't shy on speaking their minds. The discussions are also more engaging. Although, this will vary from a group to the other. If you find the right group that suits your need, you will end up connecting with your like-minded. The knowledge in which you will gain will also be huge. Apart from demonstrating your expertise by discussions and commenting, you will be exposed to new ideas and news. As a result, you will have formed solid alliances.

4. **Your Resume Will Be Up-To-Date.**

We write resumes when we are actively looking for a job. After getting a job, we forget about them. Our LinkedIn network tend to stay up to date. It will have more accurate information about us, compared to other online profiles. Many recruiters understand about this. They understand that your network will be highly accurate than your three-year-old CV.

Writing your new resume will be much easier when your LinkedIn profile is up-to date. You will just have to check your profile and know what to write, rather than starting at a black A4 page pondering where you started to where you stopped. Always be ready with an updated LinkedIn profile. Employers or recruiters can just hit on you without a 'good' notice.

5. **News and feeds From Your Industry.**

According to the latest research, the average time spent on LinkedIn network is about 4 minutes. The company has found this annoying where as a result it has devised some ways to keep you on. Among them is through the ability to customize the news that you receive daily. You daily news will inform you on some of the thing that you should consider knowing about your job. This is mainly based on your network, the types of article you share, and your industry. You can still customize your news feed or choose to get what your peers are reading.

Creating a LinkedIn Profile – What Makes a Great LinkedIn profile?

Many people sign up for a profile with LinkedIn and duplicate their resume for some ten minutes before calling it done! Although, this is not the essence of having a LinkedIn profile. You are meant to use it like a detailed resume – for networking. Such people don't capitalize on the ability to add publications, images, and videos. Publications, videos, and images makes your profile to gain legitimacy and look more attractive. **This is like personal branding. Learn how to best fill your network here:**

Picture:

Your professional headline, your name, and picture are the most time seen things on your profile. Therefore there is need to make them look professional, so that, people can recognize you when they see you in a trade show or conference. Just take a photo of you – even as much as you love your family, let them not appear in the picture.

Headline and Your Name:

As mentioned before, your headline sells you a lot. You should maximize the use of the 120 characters of your professional headline. You should describe who you serve and what you do. Furthermore, you should use your official names on your profile. You can put your nickname in brackets. This helps people to easily recognize you.

Summary:

You should capitalize on using the 2,000 characters with keywords that match the job that you are looking for. Ensure that such keywords appear seamlessly (not stashed keywords) within the summary content. You can add some media, like jpg's, YouTube videos, and screenshots of a testimonial page, among others.

Experience:

Use the experience platform to go beyond your resume. Consider sharing media like relevant presentations, images, articles quoting you, or videos. Take advantage of visuals to spruce up your LinkedIn. It makes it to look even more attractive.

Recommendations:

It is wise to get two recommendations. This is perhaps best for each of your former most important positions. It is advantageous to obtain such recommendations from most influential people in your industry. It can be about your character or how you did business with them.

Connections:

Ensure that you have at least 300 connections. This offers you with a big enough network that professionally useful to you. You should otherwise stay under 3,000 connections a point where your network "starts breaking." Connect to people you should know like family, former colleagues, experts in your industry, and fellow alumni. This will also help you in getting endorsed. Also customize your LinkedIn profile URL.

Ensure that you have filled the rest of the parts. Be creative. Update your contact information and always engage with your network. This makes you to stand out of the crowd and thus increases your chances of 'landing to the eyes' of a recruiter.

Chapter 5: Why a Personal Website Distinguishes You from the 'Crowd'

With your LinkedIn network, you still belong to a very big crowd. You still need to find unique ways of distinguishing yourself from the crowd. Creating a personal websites puts you miles ahead of other job seekers with skills that are similar to yours. Remember, that competition is stiff among job seekers. Fresh graduates share similar grades, nice resumes and cover letters, and great LinkedIn profiles. Creativity is what distinguishes them from other applicants. How can you be creative with a personal website?

A personal website showcases your unique brand. It makes you stand out from the rest of the applicants. You can still run an active blog along with your personal website. This supplements it by making it active. Linking your personal website (blog) with your social media accounts will stuff them with great content in line with your career making them attractive.

As per research, only about 7% of job applicants use personal websites. Therefore, having such a website will highly impress your potential employer. You should create your website in such a way that it has multiple elements to engage the viewer. The contents of your website should be made up of things that showcases accomplishments and professional personality. You should also include a short bio about yourself, samples of your work, a brief resume version, and a page that lists your skills. The main advantage of a personal website is the fact that you can tailor it in the way that best suits your interests and personality.

A personal website is actually among the biggest traits of your online presence. Other areas like blogs, social networks, and LinkedIn profile are still vital but the website will serve as a home base. It is the core of all the other profiles. **Here are some of the reasons on why you should create a personal website:**

1. **A Personal Website is Like a Living CV That's More Dynamic.**

Making a comparison between your resume and your personal website is like an insult to the latter. Despite the fact that you can come up with a very great resume, a personal website serves much more. It will be whatever you want it to be. A resume is typically required to adopt a certain format, whereas a website can have any theme, any format, and contain the content of your desire. You can use your website to display your projects and other work; a portfolio of your camerawork; your goals and professional success; interests and hobbies; and many other things.

2. A Personal Website Serves As An Ultimate 'Online Profile'.

The ultimate to represent yourself online is through your website. More so a self-hosted site, is far way very effective to communicate with potential recruiters, customers, employers, and other business partners of who you are. It will work way better compared to your blogs, LinkedIn network, and other social network. Self-hosted personal websites aren't the only way to go. You can still by a domain and use websites like Weebly, Striking.ly, Enthuse.me, Wordpress.com, and Wix to design your landing page.

This is actually one of the easiest way to create an awesome personal website.

3. **A Personal Website Makes You More Discoverable.**

Very many people are currently using the internet to find people. Such people are also using the internet to learn more about others. The number of those people who own personal websites in line with other social medial platforms is very low. Having a personal website highly increases your chances of being discovered when a person searches your name in Google. This also reduces the chances of another person with a name like yours misrepresenting you. Such people might end up hurting your integrity. You should claim your name online by representing yourself professionally – by your real names in all platforms.

4. **A Personal Website Improves Your Credibility Making You To 'Stand Out'.**

A personal website not only helps you to stand out of the crowd but also assists in making you more credible. You will raise your competitiveness. Consider asking your colleagues, classmates, and friends about how many of them have a personal website. You will most likely end up noticing that you are the only one with such a great evolvement. Whereas in the years to come this might change, it is ideal to take advantage now.

5. **A Personal Website Shows Your Dedication and Career Focus.**

While shaping your career, you are adding experience after experience under your focus. A personal website serves as the best place to share the experiences that you have gained through pictures and texts. You can you're the website to showcase what you are doing and your accomplishments so far. Employers, recruiters, and business partners will be able to learn about your career focus and dedication towards it.

The Following Are Among the Five Creative Personal Websites:

Designers and writers aren't the only job candidates that create personal websites. You can still create a unique personal website while in tech hubs, accounting fields, touring fields, and engineering among other departments. Some financial and accounting majors write finance blogs so as to impress their recruiting managers. Below is a list of five personal websites that you should have a look on:

1. **Tim Van Damme:**

This is a personal website with most effective features like self portrait of the job candidate. It makes him appear honest, real, and provides the readers with an impression that they have met you. This actually makes them to yearn to meet you. Click here to view the website.

2. **Samuel Reed:**

Whereas Reed doesn't tell us what he does for a living, he passively create an interactive website to tell us he is an interactive web developer. This is undeniably clever tactic. Click here to view the website. Being creative more so if you are a designer or engineer, will leave an awesome first impression.

3. **Wade Garett:**

Though his personal website Wade reveals to us that you definitely don't need to include self-portrait, state-of-the-art design skills, or animation for your work to look great. Coming up with minimalistic work does marvelous just like a handshake. You can view Wade's website here.

4. **Murage Peter:**

Peter's simple personal website shows how you can link your website with your blogs feeds. The simply curated site contain basic (but vital) information about what he does, contact, and some portfolio. You will also be able to get into his blogs via the blog feeds. Click here to view peter's personal website.

5. **Pushkar Modi:**

Pushkar's personal website mixes simplicity with an eye-catching yet simple icon. When you click through his website, his work examples and 'about me' sections aren't overdone. Best websites doesn't need to be created by flashy designers. Such sites just need to demonstrate who you are and easy to view.

You should start working on your personal website. There is plenty of online materials that will help you come up with a very unique site. In any case, you can choose to just outsource such job to a web developer who will offer you with great services.

Chapter 6: The Social Media: What Should You Know?

Employers are able to get a glimpse about our characters through sites like Google+, Twitter, SnapChat, Instagram, and Facebook. Through such social media platforms, they employers will learn about our social life and how we interact with other people. Therefore, during your job search, social media can hurt or help you. They offer the employer with more information about you outside the confines of an interview, cover letter, and a resume.

Furthermore, they offer job seekers with avenues hear about job openings, connect with former and current fellow employees, and learn about their favorite companies. As per statistics, over a third of all employers globally utilize the social media during the hiring process, while about a half of all job seekers are active on social media sites daily. As a job seeker it is good to provide consistent information about your accomplishments and yourself in your social media accounts. Never assume that employers will only check your LinkedIn network.

The main advantage is that most recruiters screen social networking sites to find information that could offer you with an advantage and not all about digging up dirt posts. Some check the overall personality of the candidate towards like. Do you complain a lot? Do you exhibit good leadership? Are you a team player? These are some of the things employers find out. Others will hire you because your social media profiles depicts a professional image. Some find great communication skills, well-rounded character, and creativity as a reason for hiring the job seeker.

This implies that as a job seeker, you shouldn't just focus on removing the contents that are inappropriate, you should work to build a great social media profile just like LinkedIn profile. Your profiles should represent your experience and skills in the workplace. 'Invisible or silent' job seekers on the social media maybe disadvantaged. Engaging on the social medial platforms improves ones search-ability and visibility. You should share expertise by engaging in group discussions, communities, and sharing content.

The Biggest Social Media Snags That Will Cost You That Job:

It is always better to be safer than being sorry. When it comes to social medial networking, always embrace safety with what you post and share. According to the CEO of Hoffeld Group, David Hoffeld, many people underestimate the reach of social media. Some assume that only the connected friends will see what they share and post. In today's world, potential customers, co-workers, future employers, and employers search online to find what type of a person you are. Therefore, being careless on the type of content that you post might end up costing you a job – even your current job. **The following are the three common social media usage mistakes that can get you fired as an employee or keep you away from getting hired as a job seeker:**

1. **Careless Posting:**

I am sure you are not hearing this for the first time. It might not be smart to dash off a tweet as you race into a meeting. A Social Recruiting Survey by Jobvite, carried out in 2014, indicates that two-thirds of recruiters negatively reconsidered their candidates due to grammar and spelling errors in their social media profiles. As such, you should learn that careless posting isn't all about 'dirty' posts. Always before hitting the 'post' button, reread the post to make sure it is not offensive in any manner. Candidates with blasphemous profiles have been negatively reconsidered by their recruiters and employers. Always avoid illegal drug references and sexual content, it tops the list of careless posting.

2. **Dishing Dirt about Bosses and Colleagues:**

Whether it is your former or current employer, you might at one point get annoyed with them. Social media makes a great place to vent and express your anger. Even when angered by colleagues. Even if you no longer work with them, you should be wary of such an act. You might be fired due to threatening the 'morale' of the company. Avoid spreading rumors about your employer. Or gossiping about your fellow employees. Most people often get fired by openly complaining about their employers and bosses online. Your boss is always more social media savvy compared to what you think of him or her.

3. **Failing to Control Your Digital Dignity:**

Many people fail to take control of their digital dignity. This also applies to job seekers. Managing your online presence isn't all about what you post on social media profiles, but also what you remove. The latter has got a huge impact. In order to manage the brand of your name successfully, consider conducting a thorough search of your professional name via Yahoo, Bing, and Google. Always never rely only on your social media privacy settings. Always mind your language and grammar. Remove each and every potentially inappropriate picture and post. You should use privacy settings to limit those who can view the information that you share. Consider setting tighter controls on such sites. You should protect your tweets and limit your content on Facebook to friends, and maybe friends of friends. If you can't say something before 10,000 people, don't say it online – that how you rate what to share and what not to share.

Be consistent on what you share on your social media sites. Also let what you share be consistent with your resume. Engage with people who share similar career goals with you. On this way, you will remain focused and use your social site in the way that best suits you and your potential employer.

Chapter 7: Does Volunteering for Vocational Services Help?

You might have a very great resume, an outstanding personal blog, and be very active in social media, but still lack that dream job. Does this mean you will sit around 'cursing' how life is unfair with you? I beg for a big NO. You can go another step of volunteering services. Who knows? You might end up revealing amazing skills that will make you get absorbed in the work force. Past surveys and research have revealed that those who volunteered had 30% better chances of getting employed than those who didn't. This is a research particularly by The Corporation for National and Community Service. It is a federal agency geared towards the promotion of volunteerism.

Why Can Volunteering Help You Get Hired?

Volunteering offers you with an opportunity to acquire knowledge and skills. You will also get a chance to interact with many people in the organization and work in a team. As a result, your boss may end up recognizing the great skills that you possess. Volunteering pays a lot; whether in the short-run or long-haul. The following are some of the reasons as to why you should volunteer:

1. **A Boost for The Long-Haul Unemployed:**

On average, an American graduate will take 13 months before getting permanent employed. Anything beyond this period might be considered "long-term" unemployed. Not that it is really long-term, but such a person will have taken a long period compared to other people. Remember that with unemployment, our social networks get weaker. Seldom will such a person get referrals. It is always wise to consider volunteering in such a scenario. You will meet new people and make new social connection ties.

2. **"The Maximum Impact" Job Search Technique:**

Volunteering has way long proven to have the maximum impact in job seeking. According to the Corporation for Nation Community Service survey's report, employers will consider those who are volunteering and interns when they want to absorb a few people in the workforce. As a volunteer, you will be among the considerations. By showing that you are hardworking and motivated, you prove that you are worth to be part of their team.

3. **Helps Job Seekers To Feel 'Needed' and Productive:**

As a job seeker, volunteering will assist in boosting your spirit. Remember, when you have applied for many jobs but without a success, you always have the feeling that nobody needs you. Although, volunteering helps you gain confident with yourself, you will find your services are much needed. It is a vital psychological benefit more so if you have been dealing with a persistent job search. The most critical element of success when seeking for a job is keeping a positive mindset.

4. **Expansion of Your Network of Contacts:**

Through volunteering, you will be able to expand your contacts network easily and effectively. Networking is a critical element of success when searching for a job. By volunteering, you will meet people whom you would have not otherwise met. As such, you will have generated an avenue to develop new relationships.

Such contacts might refer you to other employers with jobs or ultimately hire you.

What Should You Know Before Signing Up To Volunteer?

Here are the three pointers to keep back in your mind before you sign up to volunteer:

1. **Finding The Right Fit:**

You should never volunteer by default. We feel obligated and agree to help when our friends ask us for help. Remember that you are searching for a job, and as such, you should seek out volunteering jobs that are meaningful to you. Such jobs should provide you with new skills, contacts, and experience; which are closely aligned with your career goals.

2. **Treat It Like A Paid Job:**

You are seeking to volunteer because you believe you can offer great services just like the paid workforce. Hence, you should treat your volunteer job like it is a paid job. Whether you are providing your assistance for some few hours a week or for full-time basis, demonstrate serious commitment and professionalism. Find the opportunities that requires you to take on assignments that have great responsibilities. They can be board positions or leadership roles.

3. **Put The Skills and Expertise That You Have Into Use:**

You shouldn't confine your expertise and skills to yourself. Share them, show your leaders that you can help them market that new product in a different way. Help your team leader in designing that networking system. Prove to them that you are skilled in a certain way. The organization will enjoy the benefits of your unique abilities while racking up your new accomplishments.

Chapter 8: Preparing For Your First Interview

Wow! It has been a long journey from crafting resumes and cover letters, to landing your first interview. It is your biggest opportunity to express your expertise and knowledge about the job. Just like any other subsequent interviews, you will need to put some energy and time in preparing for the first interview. Understand that there is a lot of work to do to get you headed in the right tract. I am sure you have heard about body cleanliness, the right attire, eye contact, and calm face when it comes to attending the interview. Yes, you should maintain these, but also learn more about how to boost your chances of getting hired after the interview. **Follow the steps below when preparing for your first interview:**

- Inquire from your employer or recruiter if there are resources or materials that you should review before attending the interview. Also, inquire whether there is anything you should know before starting the work.

- Complete any forms that you should submit either before or during the interview. Make sure you do this ahead of time, if it is before the interview.

- Follow your new firm/company on various social networking sites and professional sites. This will help you know about any developments (either bad or good) that might be impacting the company and employer.

During The Interview Day: What Should You Know?

- You should understand that first impression can be a long-lasting impression. This not only applies to social relationships but also all the other relationships, like work. Make your first contact create a positive impression. Wear a good smile, and groom yourself in the modest way.

- You should show up early. Maybe an hour earlier for mid-day and evening interviews, or 15 minutes early for morning interviews. You should dress appropriately, depending with the job – e.g, an official suit for men for accounting jobs.

- Be polite and respectful for everyone. You shouldn't just respect the support staff, but also the administrative like guards, receptionists, and so on. Their opinions highly influence the senior staffs. Ensure they feel respected and valued.

- ➢ Know the rules of the organization. Be sure to go through their rules and regulations before attending the interview. You can call the inquiries desk of the company and request for such information. Whether it's switching off your phone or following a given routine, make sure you go by these rules.

After the interview, consider following up. You can send the interview a handwritten tank you note, just immediately after the interview. In addition to the note, you can send an email. It will help your interview to recall our name and face. Following these critical practices and preparations during your first interview can assure you of a success.

Conclusion

Thank you again for downloading this book!

I hope this book was able to help you to get resourceful information on how to get your first job.

The next step is to make your profile shine, interact with fellow workers in both social and professional media sites. You should also consider improving your personal website and dedicate yourself during the job. Remember, it isn't just a matter of getting the job, but dedicating yourself by giving it your best.

Finally, if you enjoyed this book, then I'd like to ask you for a favor, would you be kind enough to leave a review for this book on Amazon? It'd be greatly appreciated!

Click here to leave a review for this book on Amazon!

Also make sure you got the Free Bonus Article by clicking the link on the "Free Gift" Page!

Thank you and good luck!

www.ingramcontent.com/pod-product-compliance
Lightning Source LLC
Chambersburg PA
CBHW071823200526

45169CB00018B/935